Written by Heather Dakota
Designed by Daniel Jankowski

Tangerine
Press
an imprint of
SCHOLASTIC
www.scholastic.com

Scholastic and Tangerine Press and associated
logos are trademarks of Scholastic Inc

Published by Tangerine Press,
an imprint of Scholastic Inc.,
557 Broadway, New York, NY 10012

10 9 8 7 6 5 4

ISBN: 978-0-545-57092-3

Printed and bound in Guangzhou, China

Scholastic Canada, Ltd., Markham, Ontario

Table of Contents

Hello Rock Hounds!

From the ground we walk on, to the sand at the bottom of the ocean, rocks are the basic building blocks of the earth.

Plus they're awesome-looking!

The rocks in your kit are tumbled, or polished rocks. They were rough at one time, but after a lot of tumbling they are super smooth. This allows you to see some of their qualities in better detail.

ROCKS VS. MINERALS

A rock is a solid object that is made up of two or more minerals. And minerals are the building block of rocks. They are made up of the same kinds of atoms arranged in the same pattern.

Where do Rocks & Minerals Come from?

Some kinds of rocks—sedimentary and metamorphic—are formed by heat and intense pressure that squeezes dust and dirt together over millions of years. Other kinds of rocks—igneous—are formed by volcanic activity or upheaval of the Earth's crust.

Rock Experts

A **paleontologist** studies ancient life and ecosystems. This scientist finds a lot of his specimens in rocks.

A **field geologist** makes maps, looks at geological activity in different areas, and monitors the environment.

An **engineering geologist** is an expert in rock strength and in what makes up the soil. He or she helps other professionals build bridges, roads, dams, and tunnels.

Petroleum geologists search for and help mine some of the Earth's resources, including minerals, oil, natural gas, and coal.

Environmental geologists test water and soil for pollution and toxic chemicals.

geophysicists study all of the physical forms of the Earth, including rocks!

5

Rock Cycle

As time goes by, rocks can change form, from igneous to sedimentary, to metamorphic and back again!

Extrusive

IGNEOUS

Crystallization

Magma

Melt

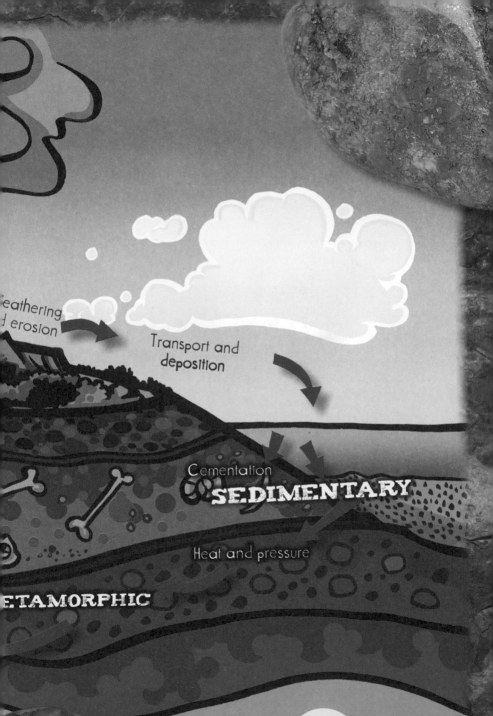

Weathering
and erosion

Transport and
deposition

Cementation

SEDIMENTARY

Heat and pressure

METAMORPHIC

Minerals 101

Minerals are the building blocks of rocks. They are made up of the same kinds of atoms arranged in the same orderly pattern.

PROPERTIES OF MINERALS

A property is a distinctive feature, like your fingerprints. Properties are what makes a mineral different from the other minerals. Thank goodness, or this rock party might be kind of boring!

ROCK HOUNDS USE MANY DIFFERENT PROPERTIES TO HELP THEM IDENTIFY MINERALS:

COLOUR - What colour does a mineral appear to be in ordinary light?

STREAK - If you drag a mineral across a streak plate, what coloured mark does it leave behind?

LUSTER - How does a mineral reflect light? Does it look shiny or dull? Greasy or waxy?

TRANSPARENCY - Can light shine through the rock?

CRYSTAL SYSTEM - How are the atoms in the mineral arranged?

SPECIFIC GRAVITY - How dense is the mineral compared to water?

HARDNESS - Can the mineral scratch other rocks?
Hint: Do not try this with the rocks from this kit. You might ruin them!

CLEAVAGE - How does your mineral break apart? Will it break smoothly along a straight line?
Hint: Again, don't try this with the rocks from this kit!

COMMON TYPES OF MINERALS

So far, more than 4,000 minerals have been found and every year new ones are discovered. Don't worry–you don't need to know them all to be a good rock hound. Only a few dozen are common within the rocks found in the Earth's crust. That means the rocks you'll find in your backyard or at the park should have common minerals in them that you can identify.

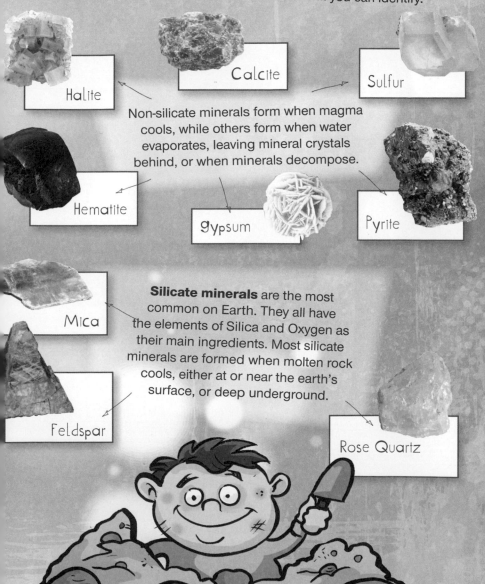

Halite

Calcite

Sulfur

Non-silicate minerals form when magma cools, while others form when water evaporates, leaving mineral crystals behind, or when minerals decompose.

Hematite

gypsum

Pyrite

Mica

Silicate minerals are the most common on Earth. They all have the elements of Silica and Oxygen as their main ingredients. Most silicate minerals are formed when molten rock cools, either at or near the earth's surface, or deep underground.

Feldspar

Rose Quartz

Igneous Rocks

Igneous rocks are called fire rocks. They can be formed underground or above ground. When melted rock, called magma, deep inside the earth becomes trapped in small pockets and begins to cool, igneous rock is formed. It can also be formed when volcanoes erupt, causing magma to rise above the Earth's surface, called lava. When the lava cools above ground, igneous rock is formed.

PROPERTIES OF IGNEOUS ROCK

1. Igneous rocks have a crystalline structure, which sometimes can only be seen under a powerful microscope. These crystals can be quite large.

2. Igneous rocks are hard.

3. Igneous rocks can be very lustrous (shiny) when they are cut or polished.

4. Some igneous rocks contain empty spaces. These are formed by bubbles in the hot lava they formed of, particularly if the lava cools quickly.

scoria

Common Types of Igneous Rocks

obsidian

pumice

granite

Sedimentary Rocks

For millions of years, little pieces of the Earth (think igneous and metamorphic rocks) have been eroded away, broken down, or worn away by water and wind. These little bits of Earth—called sediments—were washed downstream where they settled to the bottom of rivers, lakes, and oceans. Layer after layer of sediments were deposited on top of each other and are pressed down more and more over time, until the bottom layers turn into solid rock. And you know what? New sedimentary rock is being formed right now...but it happens slowly and over millions of years.

PROPERTIES OF SEDIMENTARY ROCK

1. Sedimentary rocks have definite layers, visible to the naked eye.

2. Since sedimentary rocks consist of a lot of little particles, most of them do not have crystalline structures.

3. Most sedimentary rocks have a matte, or dull surface.

4. Sedimentary rocks are soft and easy to scratch or crush.

5. Some sedimentary rocks contain fossils.

Common Types of Sedimentary Rocks

Limestone

conglomerate

shale

Metamorphic Rocks

Metamorphic rocks are rocks that change from one form to another. These rocks were originally igneous or sedimentary. When igneous or sedimentary rocks are under lots of pressure, tremendous heat builds up. This heat causes a chemical change and they morph into a new rock with different characteristics.

PROPERTIES OF METAMORPHIC ROCK

1. Metamorphic rocks usually have a layered structure.

2. Parallel streaks of shimmering flakes of mica can be found in the rock.

3. Metamorphic rocks will break up into flat plates when broken.

4. Most metamorphic rocks are hard, but reactions can occur when certain acids are dropped on them.

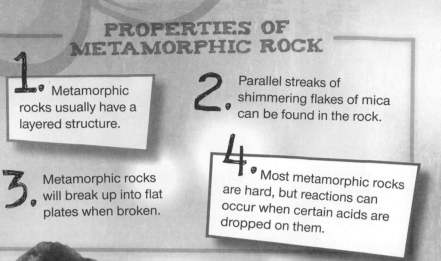

schist

Common Types of Metamorphic Rocks

gneiss

All About Gems

Many minerals form beautiful crystals, but the most prized of all are the gemstones. A gem is a mineral that has been cut and polished—the more rare, the better. Even with more than 4,000 minerals in existence, fewer than 100 of them are used to create gems. Popular gemstones include: diamond, ruby, and emerald.

Uncut gemstones are rather plain-looking. It's only when they are cut and polished that they become valued.

Precious Gemstones

Diamonds are made of carbon atoms and are the hardest natural substance found on Earth. They are formed under a lot of pressure, hundreds of miles underground. You can only find them in a few locations around the world.

Rubies are formed from the mineral corundum. The red colour is caused by traces of the element chromium.

Emeralds are formed of the mineral beryl, which contains a mix of the elements beryllium, aluminum, silicon, and oxygen. Emeralds are always green, but the colour can vary, depending on the trace amounts of chromium and vanadium. Different trace elements produce different colours. Beryl can also form the semiprecious stone, aquamarine.

Sapphires are also formed from corundum, but are mixed with other elements like iron and titanium. Sapphires come in many different colours— blue, green, orange, yellow, pink and more!

GEMSTONES ARE CLASSIFIED BY THEIR PHYSICAL PROPERTIES, LIKE THOSE LISTED ON PAGES 8 AND 9.

Rock Polishing 101

As you've been reading, rocks and minerals come in all kinds of different colours and patterns. Polishing them to a smooth shininess brings out their natural beauty.

WAYS TO POLISH ROCKS

If you've ever been to the beach or a lake, you've probably picked up smooth, rounded, and sometimes shiny, rocks. The ocean and lake waters are natural rock tumblers. As rocks are rolled by the waves and rubbed against the sand and each other, their edges and corners are filed down. Rock tumblers and hand polishing are the best way to polish your rough rocks. However, both of these methods take a long time (4 to 6 weeks).

DON'T HAVE A TUMBLER?
TRY THESE D.I.Y. TECHNIQUES
TO POLISH YOUR ROCKS.

Vaseline (petroleum jelly). This works the same way as the other techniques. Clean your rough rocks and let them dry. Add the Vaseline with your fingers. Rub the Vaselined rock with a piece of denim, cotton cloth, or old towel. You might need to redo this from time to time, to keep your rock shiny.

Clear nail polish. Clean your rough stones with soap and hot water. Let dry. After the rocks are dry, brush on clear nail polish. Try not to go over the area in which you have already brushed or you will streak the polish. Let dry. You can add another coat if you want to add more shine. Your rocks will be shiny, but still have that rough look.

Mineral or Baby Oil. Clean your stones with hot water and soap. After they dry, coat with a bit of baby oil or mineral oil. You can also polish them with an emery cloth, denim, cotton cloth, or an old towel if you want a smoother look, (see above).

Emery cloth or wet/dry sandpaper. This can take weeks of elbow grease but is a quieter option than tumbling. Start with a coarse grit cloth or paper and slowly work your way down to a f grit. When the stone is almost smoot switch to denim for an even smoothe and polished look.

SOME THINGS TO CONSIDER BEFORE POLISHING YOUR OWN ROCKS.

1. Make sure your rocks are about ½ to 2 cm in diameter.

2. Soft rocks such as calcite, marble, obsidian, and fluorite are soft and shape quickly in a rock tumbler. Harder rocks, such as jasper, agate, petrified wood, and quartz take more time to polish. Check the Mohs Hardness scale before you start to see what you're in for—the harder the rock, the longer polishing it will take.

3. Pick rocks that have colours and patterns that you like. Test this by rubbing a bit of water on your rock to see the colours. Your polished rock will look similar.

TAKING CARE OF YOUR POLISHED ROCKS

Care for your polished rocks with a little bit of mineral oil rubbed onto your rock with a piece of denim, cotton cloth, or an old towel. You can also use a jeweller cleaning cloth or eyeglass cleaning tissues to remove fingerprints. Do not wash your rocks as they may lose their shine.

In 1812, Friedrich Mohs developed a hardness scale for rocks. His scale ranged from 1 (soft) to 10 (hard) and measured how well rocks could scratch one another.

1	2	3	4	5	6	7	8	9	10
Talc	Gypsum	Calcite	Fluorite	Apatite	Ortho-clase	Quartz	Topaz	Corun-dum	Diamond

MAKE A KID-POWERED ROCK TUMBLER. SEE PAGES 20-21.

Make Your Own Kid-powered Rock Tumbler

You can make your own tumbler out of a few household items. But be prepared for Lots and Lots of shaking!

THINGS YOU'LL NEED:

- Large plastic container with a screw-on lid.
- coarse sand
- medium grit sand
- fine grit sand
- water
- selection of rocks

WHAT TO DO:

1. Take your container and add enough coarse sand to cover the rocks.

2. Fill the container about ⅓ full of water to make a gritty slurry.

3. Secure the lid. It needs to be very tight, so it doesn't come loose when you shake the container.

4. Shake and roll the tumbler vigorously for 1 week. You can do this while you're watching TV, riding in the car, or waiting around.

5. Then, check to see how the polishing is coming along. If it looks good, replace the coarse sand with medium grit sand and start the process over again.

6. After another week, check your rocks again. If they are smoothing up nicely, repeat this process with the fine grit sand, until your rocks have the smoothness that you want.

Electric Rock Tumblers are a fun way to polish your rocks. It still takes about a month and the tumbler has to run all day, every day, but you get beautifully polished rocks. The tumbler itself costs between $40 and $100. And don't forget to add in the cost of the special sand and electricity to run the machine, which will be about $5 to $25 for each batch of rocks.

Note: The amount of sand will depend on how many rocks you want to polish. You'll want to cover the rocks with the sand.

Rock Collecting 101

Rock collecting is a fun and easy hobby. Why? Because rocks are everywhere. You could collect them for years and years and still have thousands more waiting for you to discover.

ROCK COLLECTING IS A SAFE HOBBY AS LONG AS YOU FOLLOW A FEW GUIDELINES. IF YOU GO OUT ROCK COLLECTING, ALWAYS TAKE A BUDDY. AND DON'T COLLECT AROUND OLD MINES OR QUARRIES. NEVER ENTER TUNNELS OR HOLES! THESE ARE OFTEN UNSTABLE AND COULD COLLAPSE.

LET'S GET ROCKIN'

Collect clean, fresh specimens.

Make a label that has the name of the rock and the location where it was collected.

Assign a number to each rock.

Record in a notebook the name, location where you found it, and number of the rock.

Paint a small white rectangle on each rock, and write the rock's number on it.

Find a rock collecting mentor, someone who knows all about rock collecting and can guide you. Don't know anyone like that? Ask your parents to help you. Or ask at your school, museum, or library. There's bound to be someone who can help get you started.

What kind of Rock is it?

Here are a few tips to help you identify common rocks that you might find in your backyard or on vacation. The kinds of rocks included in your kit are just a few of the kinds of rocks out there. They are the more common varieties, but it is possible that you will try to identify a rock which is not on the list.

Identification of Igneous Rocks

grain Size	Usual Colour	Description	Rock Type
fine	dark	glassy appearance	Obsidian
fine	light	many small bubbles	Pumice
fine	dark	many large bubbles	Scoria
fine or mixed	dark	has no quartz	Basalt
coarse	light wide	range of color and grain size	granite
coarse	dark	dense; always has olivine	Peridotite

Identification of Sedimentary Rocks

grain Size	Usual Colour	Description	Rock Type
coarse	white to brown	clean quartz,	Sandstone
mixed	mixed Colours	mixed rocks and sediment, round rocks in finer sediment matrix	Conglomerate
fine	gray	splits in layers	Shale
fine	black	black; burns with tarry smoke	Coal
fine	white, gray, and light brown	dissolves in rainwater; under pressure can turn to marble	Limestone
coarse or fine	pinkish or white	has a pearly luster	Dolomite rock
coarse	light brown, white, to dark brown	mostly pieces of fossils and shells	Coquina

Identification of Metamorphic Rocks

grain Size	Usual Colour	Description	Rock Type
fine	light grey	very soft; greasy feel	Soapstone
fine	light or dark green, brown, terracotta	soft; breaks along a flat plane	Slate
coarse	flat and shiny	often has large crystals	Schist
coarse	white or light	gray soft; used for sculptures	Marble
coarse	mixed	banded	gneiss
coarse	many colours	quartz crystals	Quartzite

Field #1: Experiment

Chemical Weathering

As hard as they are, rocks don't last forever. There are many ways that they can be changed.

This change is called weathering. There are two main types of weathering. One is chemical weathering, rocks and minerals are exposed to water, acids and gases that dissolve or react to some of the minerals in the rock. When this reaction happens, new compounds are formed and these sediments are dissolved or washed away. Try it yourself:

THINGS YOU'LL NEED:

- two pieces of limestone, calcite, chalk, or quartz
- lemon juice
- vinegar

WHAT TO DO:

1. Put a few drops of lemon juice on the first set of rock samples.

2. Put a few drops of vinegar on the second set of rock samples.

3. Listen carefully as you add the drops.

BIOLOGICAL WEATHERING

This type of weathering is caused by living organisms, like tree roots and burrowing animals. Tree roots can grow into the cracks of a rock.

GOOD TO KNOW

Lemon juice and vinegar are weak acids. The lemon juice contains citric acid and the vinegar contains acetic acid. These acids can dissolve rocks that contain calcium carbonate (which the rock samples do). If you got a bubbling or fizzing effect on the limestone, calcite, and chalk, you did the experiment just right! You shouldn't have had any reaction on the quartz. Why do you think that is? If you guessed that it doesn't have calcium carbonate, you're absolutely right!

Mechanical Weathering

Now that you know about chemical weathering,
let's look at mechanical weathering.

This occurs when rocks are broken down by changes in temperature or bumping up against other rocks. When rocks are heated and then cooled, the minerals within them expand and contract at different rates. Cracks and breaks occur. If water gets into the cracks, it can break the rock apart, especially if it freezes! Unlike chemical weathering, the chemical composition of the rock and sediment remains the same. Mechanical weathering continues until the rock falls apart. Chemical weathering and mechanical weathering can happen at the same time.

THINGS YOU'LL NEED:

- Plaster of Paris
- water
- a small balloon
- 2 – 250ml (½ pint) empty milk boxes, opened up
- access to a freezer

WHAT TO DO:

1. Fill the balloon with water until it is the size of a ping-pong ball. Tie a knot at the end.

2. Mix the Plaster of Paris with water until the mixture looks like thick yogurt. Pour half of the plaster in each milk carton.

3. Push the balloon into the plaster of one milk carton until it is about .5 cm (¼ in.) under the surface. Hold the balloon there until the plaster sets enough so the balloon doesn't move.

4. Let the plaster harden for about 1 hour.

5. Put both milk cartons in the freezer overnight.

6. Remove the containers.

GOOD TO KNOW
The container with the plaster and the balloon should have cracked as the water in the balloon froze.

Why?
When water freezes, it expands. That's why the rocks break apart when water seeps into cracks in a rock and freezes.

Make a Sedimentary Layer Model

You've seen how to destroy rocks, so let's turn that around and start making a rock.

THINGS YOU'LL NEED:

- small clear plastic water bottle and cap
- gravel
- sand
- chalk powder or Plaster of Paris
- water
- piece of paper
- scissors
- measuring spoons

Warning! Get parent to hel you with the scissors and Plaster of Paris.

WHAT TO DO:

1. Shape the paper into a funnel with an opening at the bottom and secure with tape.

2. Place your funnel into the opening of the water bottle.

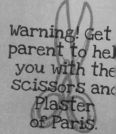

3. Measure out 75 ml (5 tablespoons) of sand and pour it into the bottle.

4. Next comes the gravel. Measure 75 ml (5 tablespoons) of gravel and pour that into the bottle.

5. Lastly, measure 75 ml (5 tablespoons) of chalk powder or Plaster of Paris and pour that into the bottle.

6. Pour water into the bottle until it is half full.

7. Screw on the cap and shake the bottle for about 20 seconds to mix verything up.

8. Set the bottle down and leave it alone for a few minutes. Watch what happens.

GOOD TO KNOW

When you shook up the bottle, all of the particles of material were mixed together in the water, just like what happens in rivers, lakes, and oceans. When you set the bottle down, the particles sank to the bottom and arranged themselves by weight and size. The particles that were heaviest sank to the bottom and the lightest particles rose to the top.

Voila! Sediment!

Trivia and Fun Facts

Feldspar makes up more than 50 per cent of the Earth's crust.

Quartz is one of the most common minerals on Earth.

In Mesopotamia around 5000 BCE, people used turquoise to make beads.

Ancient Egyptians used powdered Lapis Lazuli as eye shadow.

The largest pure-gold nugget was found in Australia in 1869. It weighed 70.8 kg (156 lbs).

Geodes are dull balls of igneous or sedimentary rock on the outside, but they contain beautiful crystals inside.

Rocks from space are called Meteorites.

The largest single quartz crystal was about 6m (20 ft.) long and weighed more than 43.5 tonnes (48 tons).

The oldest rocks on Earth are found in northwestern Canada near Great Slave Lake. The Gneiss rocks are approximately 3.5 billion years old.

TOP 10 MOST EXPENSIVE DIAMONDS IN THE WORLD.

1. The Koh-I-Noor Diamond -
   clear diamond, 105 carats, price: priceless

2. The Sancy Diamond - pale yellow diamond, 55.23 carats, price: priceless

3. The Cullinan Diamond - clear diamonds, 3,106.75 carats, price: $400 million

4. The Hope Diamond - blue diamond, 45.52 carats, price: $350 million

5. De Beers Centenary Diamond - clear, 273.85 carats, price: $100 million

6. The Steinmetz Pink Diamond - vivid pink diamond, 59.6 carats, price: $25 million

7. Wittelsbach-Graff Diamond - blue diamond, 35.36 carats, price: $16.4 million

8. The Heart of Eternity Diamond - vivid blue diamond, 27.64 carats, price: $16 million

9. The Moussaieff Red Diamond - red diamond, 5.11 carats, price: $7 million

10. The Allnatt Diamond - vivid yellow diamond, 101.29 carats, $3 million

The Hopewell Rocks, AKA: Flower Pot rocks are sedimentary rocks formations in the Bay of Fundy. The rocks have been eroded away by the mechanical weathering of the tides over millions of years. When the tides are out, you can see the weathered rock.

Glossary

atom - a small particle of matter

cementation - the hardening of sediments. This is the last stage of formation of sedimentary rocks

composition - what something is made of

compound - formed by combining parts

crystallization - caused to form crystals

deposition - the action or process of depositing

elements - any of more than 100 substances that consist of atoms of only one kind and that cannot be separated into simpler substances

erosion - the action or process of breaking something down

extrusive - formed by coming out of the earth in a melted state

gemologists - professionals who inspect, grade, and appraise gemstones

geologist - an expert in the history and structure of the Earth

hypothesis - something not proven by assumed to be true for purposes of further study and investigation

Igneous - a type of rock that is formed by cooling magma or lava

lapidary - a person who cuts and polishes precious stones

lava - hot liquid rock that has reached the Earth's surface

magma - hot liquid rock beneath the Earth's surface

matter - anything that takes up space

metamorphic - changed into a more compact form by pressure, heat, and water

mineral - a solid substance that is always made up of the same kind of atoms arranged in an orderly pattern

particle - a very small quantity or piece

property - a distinctive quality or characteristic

sedimentary - formed by very small pieces and cementing

slurry - a watery mix of mud, lime, or Plaster of Paris

symmetrical - having or showing balanced size, shape, and position of parts

transparent - allowing light to pass through

weathering - a mechanical or chemical process that transforms rocks and minerals